An Address To King Cotton

Eugene Pelletan

KPT

AN ADDRESS

TO

ING COTTON

BY ⟨268288⟩
QP 42238

EUGÈNE PELLETAN

Author of several Works on America.

TRANSLATED BY

LEANDER STARR.

TS.

PUBLISHED

H. DE MAREIL, EDITOR OF THE MESSAGER FRANCO-AMERICAIN
51, LIBERTY STREET, NEW YORK.

———

1863

AN

ADDRESS TO KING COTTON.

SIRE :

 ̔ou nave committed a wrong act.   It is not everything to be a
, even with only a bale for a throne : one must also be faithful to the
titution.   I talk to you without flattery, and as I have broached the
ct, I shall go to the end of the reel.   But first let me throw a retrospec-
glance at the past.
in the 16th century, at the time when Thomas Morus wrote his Utopia.....
this is going too far back.   Suppose in the 17th century, while
on was elaborating his kingdom of Salente, a seer had spoken to
effect : "I have found a telescope that plunges into time as the other
ins space !   But my glass shows me something still more marvellous
the Utopia of Morus, or the Salente of the archbishop of Cambrai.
yond the setting sun, on the other side of the Atlantic, I see a tract of
nent twenty times as large as France, with two sides on two oceans,
ne looking toward Europe, the other toward Asia.   One might deem it
iddle of the world, the central empire.   At the first glance it
s an uncouth territory, overgrown with jungles and sub-
ed by swamps.   Some sixty rivers, nameless as yet, flow at random,
ig one's path in all directions.   There are no inhabitants but the wolf
he bison, save here and there a man if we may thus call carnivorous
ires, who after six thousand years of reflection have been unable to
re any other talent than that of lighting a fire at night by which to
their food.
d yet this chaotic soil, rude as the deluge left it, will be chosen by good
banished from England on account of a dubious point of biblical inter-
tion, as an asylum for themselves, their wives and children, so : that
may have a right to interpret the Bible in their own way.
w many will they number ?   A mere handful of men, barely a boat
  They will sing a psalm upon landing in this new hemisphere and
with a pious glance at the snow-covered soil, they will take up the
x.
y will have but one ambition ; prayer and labor—prayer in order to
the life to come and labor to gain time for prayer.   After clearing the
rd they will bravely attack the barriers of the untrodden forest ; they
eliver the soil, buried and imprisoned beneath a night of verdure ; they
show it openly to heaven and heaven will let its dews and har-
descend upon it.
ward, ever advancing, go ahead, will be the motto of this heroic race.

This rugged land conceals the germ of kindly usefulness. It awaits bu word from man to pass into a state of civilization. There are immense la or rather seas, destined to create a coasting trade ; and the sixty rivers though obstacles at the outset, will become later great highways, bind together the various centres of population. And at last the great Mis sippi, the "father of waters," will draw all these navigable streams in course of a thousand leagues and bear them along in triumph with th fleets to the Gulf of Mexico.

And they will advance ever and ever westward, (for civilization foll the course of the sun,) and wherever they go they will find the same clim as in England ; the same winter and the same summer. They may beli if they will, that they have brought the seasons of Europe with them, s in the folds of their cloaks. They will be able to carry to their new h the productions of the old country; their wheat and hemp; their gardens orchards. They will be able to carry with them the companions of their ca life,—the ox, the horse, the dog, the sheep, &c. Men and flocks will lan families, and after a voyage of fifteen hundred leagues, they will seem have passed to the other shore of their own country.

II.

But a day will come when this colony, scarcely a century old, born labor and multiplied by labor, will wish to rise and rank as a nation, manage its own household. Then it will have to struggle desperately the mother-country, the first maritime power, and perhaps also the military power of Europe. But North America will have confidence in destiny. An inward voice will say to her : "Do what you fear to do ! ter the strife with nature, comes the strife with England. This will be changing the battlefield, and America will win the day. She will f England to sign the certificate of birth of the United States, and on the row the Atlantic will bear for the first time a flag with but thirteen s as yet."

I do not know how or by what secret instinct more powerful than reflec the American republic will find the most perfect form of government to cupy and rule half a continent ; but it will be found, whether at the or the second trial it matters little. Man, master of himself in everyt concerning the individual ; a common independence in all his acts regar his religious existence ; corporate sovereignty in everything of interes the people constituted as a state ; and lastly the confederacy as the supr umpire in all matters in which the states are jointly interested, this is American Constitution. In other words it is social life copied from na and written down upon paper.

The sovereign people will delegate power to it, still always retai their sovereignty. Administration, juries, legislation, government an power will emanate from the people to be restored to the people at the piration of their mandate.

Public election will constitute in some degree a distilling apparatus w will be constantly at work, and through which public opinion will eva ate in power. In addition to all this a president will be elected who rule over thirty millions of men for the low su n of one hundred and two thousand francs per annum and who will live n a cottage. At the en his term he will disappear in the crowd and take to sowing wheat clover.

n admirable organization is this, producing at the same time a double
rement of expansion and concentration ; an expansion colonising from
out, a concentration binding the various colonies together in one united
atry.   And thus the American Constitution will surround liberty with as
y breastworks as there may be states in the confederacy, so that of all
ossibilities the most impossible would be the hypothesis of a Yankee
ar with his foot upon the corpse of the republic striving to mount to
reign power.

s American emigration clears away what will be called simply a terri-
, the starry constitution will travel westward almost step by step in
pany with the nomadic labor of the pioneer.   When this new territory
have attained a legal amount of population, the constitution will take
of it at once and incorporate it in the family of states ; and one more
will shine upon the banner of the republic.

ie confederacy will thus grow constantly from these cuttings, embrac-
all the newly-hatched colonies in the West in the simple bonds of a
v that will protect all the integral parts of the Union without ever be-
ble to hold any one of them in bondage.   Still who will believe it ?
model constitution will result in a degree from chance or if you prefer
m a compromise.   A hidden destiny will doubtless dictate it, as though
d one day to support a world.

III.

berty alone possesses creative power ; and thanks to liberty the Ameri
epublic will expand in space—man will outstrip time in speed   When
welth or the fifteenth son of the same father reaches the age of reason,
ill harness up a wagon and load it with the emigrant's Spartan outfit ;
embrace his family and drive away.

here will he go ?   To the great West.   After picking out a suitable
of public land, he will attack the forest with his ax, sow his corn in
aring, and build his log cabin on the outskirts of the wood.   When he
aised a roof above his head, he will think that two heads might rest
as well as one ; after this reflection he will light his pipe, get into the
e, and return to the village of his childhood.

will go there to seek a companion, and will marry the first comer.   He
draw blindly in the lottery, but he will always find the spirit of order
abor.   Virtue is the only dowry of America's daughters.   As to any
dowry, it will not be thought of.   How are the children to live ?
will emigrate in their turn.

soon as the pioneer receives the nuptial blessing, he will return to his
abin, taking his wife with him : but this time he will take furniture
attle along.   Sometime later, a traveling missionary sent to spread
ospel in the wilderness, will check his horse before a newly built farm
, at the sight of a swarm of little ones playing on the threshold under
tico of fragrant vines.

n draws near to man in the chemistry of society, as one atom attracts
er, in another order of composition.   A new cabin will spring up in
eighborhood of the one already built, for reasons both of sympathy and
.   Soon manufacturing industry will compete with agriculture.   The
smith will light his forge fire by the side of the homestead, to hammer
s ploughshares ; the wheelwright will follow the blacksmith, and then
rpenter, and so on, until the tailor arrives. Agriculture disperses and

manufactures concentrate. The village will owe its birth to the latter. N
I designate the first public edifice to be built with the savings of the com
nity ? It will be a schoolhouse.

And why should it not ? Is not the Bible the worship of the Protest
pioneer ? Does not his piety come from reading ? Is it not the first
dence of a free citizen of a free country to be able to read at least his ne
paper ? Religion will first lodge in the schoolhouse : but in course of t
it will have a separate residence : a church with its steeple] will arise
the church bells will tell the winds of the birth of a new community.

Thould there exist any local circumstances favorable to its developem
the community will grow almost magically. What was but a village
change into a little town, then into an ordinary sized town, and at last
a great city, the metropolis of a hundred thousand souls. A hundred th
and, what am I saying, *four* hundred thousand, and all this, within the
of one man, and upon a soil where only yesterday the buffalo browsed
liberty.

What will it become then, when steam gives American civilization a s
equal to its aspirations? Everything to be done thenceforth,—agricultura
industrial—must be done by machinery. The soil must be tilled, and
harvest reaped by machinery. The entire surface of the earth will bec
one immense machine, ever panting with labor. Armed with steam p
North America will defy impossibilities, and even attempt to imitate m
cles. For example, a railroad one thousand leagues in length, will be
down, and the engine darting through the immensity of space, will call
with a shrill whistle, the yet buried phantom of future cities, and these
ies, will spring from the ground at the call of steam, to take their places
the sunlight.

IV.

The news of this great prosperity and its unprecedented rapidity will cr
the sea, and the people of the old world, deprived of their share in the
will cross the Atlantic, and cover the predestined land of the West with
living alluvium. It will be a crusade of labor. All the energy of Euro
(for it takes strong nerve to submit to expatriation), will thus concur
swell the energy of America ; and from their combination, and from the
tion and reaction of their double electricity a new and unexpected race
arise ; one that will grow an inch in each generation.

The Saxon element will prove the richest soil, and will give the deep
impress to this new civilization. It will lead foreign emigrants to the w
ship of labor and of liberty, the parent of labor. It will fulfil a purp
similar to the great tun at Heidelberg, into which new wine was pou
each year, that it might at once partake of the nature of the old. Then
being hitherto unknown will appear ; the last type of man ; man master
himself ; man his own sovereign, his own policeman, his own priest : th
absolute, the Yankee. He will not wait for the government to protect h
he will protect himself, nor for the State to enrich him, he will make
own fortune ; nor wait for the government to designate his religion
the budget, for he will choose his own religion himself, supporting it
of his savings.

DThere will be no more oppression, either of conscience or any other s
cies ; no oppression of one class by another, or of all classes of society b
permanent army. North America will only have an army for appeara

..e, consisting at most of twelve thousand men, disseminated in little
..nds over the entire extent of her territory. There, there will be no un-
..asant traces of the past, no law of primogeniture, no exclusive acade-
..es, no embroidery of distinctive rank, no crosses and decorations, no
..nging courtiers, no sinecure officers, no charity under the name of re-
...rd. Men will be estimated at their real value ; nothing will be respect-
..save work and money—the incarnation of labor ; but it will have to be
..ned by the sweat of one's brow, for the *Dolce far niente* will be looked
..on in America as a robbery committed upon society in general. On the
..er hand every sort of trade will become glorious. Work, no matter in
..at manner ; be what you list, bootmaker, tailor, gardener or lawyer ;
..ose your own calling, provided that you loyally furnish your tribute of
..or. In America every trade has its own nobility ; the President of the
..ublic may be chosen from a carpenter's shop.

.. seer might have spoken thus two centuries since ; but had he done so,
..would have been treated as a visionary, he might perhaps even been
..licly burnt, as duly attainted and convicted of dealings with the evil
... And still the prophecy would have been but an anticipation of the
..lity ; for if a nation has ever existed in the universe that has done honor
..he species, that nation is North America, with its motto, "God and Lib-
..y," and which, with the Bible in one hand and the ax in the other, has
..red the surface of a world in a twinkling, and shown man in all the
..udor of virtue.

..n the very air of this new country, there is an indefinable breathing of
..juvenile nature, an inexplicable strength that expands one's chest, an
..uberant healthfulness in its exhalations that fortifies both body and
..d. There is in the daily labors of the pioneer, alone with Providence,
..mething of religion which in a manner elevates the soul to the mountain
..s. In this poetical and odorous laboratory of agriculture, with no roof
..the heavens, no boundary save the horizon, there exists a continual re-
..blance to the Infinite, reminding man of his ultimate destiny.

..ut while the American race was growing great by labor, what were
..doing, Sire, on your part, you and your partisans? You were looking
..ously upon the constantly increasing prosperity of your Western neigh-
..for whom you felt a fraternal friendship like that of Cain. You were
..spiring secretly in order to establish the kingdom of cotton and the
..remacy of cotton shirts upon the ruins of the republic.

..ut you were so unfortunate as to have been born too near the sun, in a
..ny of bad origin whose godfather was the prince of libertines, and
..se godmother was the scum of the jacobite army. The first viceroy
..ed by Locke's constitution to the rule of Carolina was, I believe, Gener-
..Monk, a bedizened traitor who sold the liberty of his country for money.
..r ancestor was a scoundrel, Sire ; and you have not disgraced your
..ent.

V.

..Why then do you wish to rend asunder this splendid American republic
..joy and glory of humanity ? We must know it for the instruction of
..century, and that man may learn to do his duty alway despite every-
..g. The American Constitution certainly compassed the ultimatum of
..dom ; but it lacked courage in one clause, and this weakness was des-
..d one day to compromise the very existence of the confederacy. Provi-

dence does not allow evil to remain in what is good. When it has o
entered it acts like the lead in a wound; either the wound expels
missile or the metal ag aravates the wound until death ensues.

When America became possessed of liberty slavery already existed i
portion of the country: but the day that she solemnly proclaimed be
God the right of every man to happiness, she should have placed the re
ty in harmony with the principle, without futile distinctions. She
afraid of justice and dared neither abolish nor recognize slavery; she
not even dare name it. It was tacitly permitted as though a question
this nature could be passed over and avoided in silence; but in truth its
lution was entrusted to time.

But time only accepts such drafts by doubling the debt of the past.
longer emancipation was put off the more aggravated did the difficulty
come, and to you, Sire, is due the credit of the spread of this scourge.
very moment that some poor devil, accidentally but honestly, found an
fernal machine to pick cotton, you transformed the South into a cot
plantation. And in order to cultivate this plantation the special labou
the slave became necessary.

What is a slave? Those black metaphysicians who wish to elevate
vitude into a theory in order to quiet their consciences, give us such a
tic idyl of negro existence that we needs must re-assert the truth in
euphemism "involuntary labor."

Slavery is thus termed so as to spare the delicacy of "ears polite."
yourself, Sire, posted as you are in the matter, never call it except b
periphrase. In your code, if I am not mistaken, you designate it the
culiar institution." Barefaced as you are in reality, you at least show
manity in this title; and in this you imitate the inquisition which alw
dealt in euphemisms toward its victims; thus the torture room was ter
the "casa santa" and upon the stake was inscribed the word "misericord

But what is a slave? A slave is a man robbed of his soul, he and
race, until the end of posterity; a man doomed from father to son to t
with the brains and will through the volition of another; a man
vested of the first sacred right of man; to wit, individuality; a be
changed from his nature; in a word an artificial monster, a moral enn
undeserving of the deprivation. The church castrates the child to n
him sing well, but you, Sire, you castrate him that he may pick your
ton. This is the only difference.

If in order to render a man a slave it were necessary to cut off one of
legs or arms, the sight of the knife and of the stump would certainly in
end excite pity; and pity once raised what might not ensue.

But the white man, having tired of cutting and maiming, finally wis
to leave the negro entire. In order to transform a man into an autom
it suffices to take away his soul gently; and as this requires neither k
nor surgical operation, as it causes neither outcries nor bloodshed
world looks on quietly. After all it is only a metaphysical murder c
mitted in the realms of the invisible. We do not see or touch it and
sleep with a sound conscience. And yet, whatever may be said in
country of yellow fever or sugar cane, there is more cruelty in mutila
him physically. Place the one against the other and were fate to sum
us to choose we should certainly prefer the loss of a leg to that of ou
telligence, we had rather lose an arm than our will.

Servitude in common with every human institution has its own lo
Emanating from barbarity it leads from cruelty to cruelty, as result foll
result in reasoning.

You feed the slave while in infancy (I had nearly added while in

also ; but forced labor beneath a tropical sun rarely allows him to
w old) therefore the negro must earn by his daily labor not only his
ent but his past sustenance ; but the negro has no interest to stimulate
to work, so you supply its place with the whip. This is your idea of
perfection of labor ; but this is not all : discipline must be maintained
his band of scourged creatures, giddy and noisy as children
he raw hide teaches him to keep order and to love his master or mis-
s. Both in France and in England by a braminical species of law cruel-
 animals is punishable ; but in America the skin of man is not held in
 high esteem. There the negro's blood is shed upon the slightest pro-
ation, for a petty blunder.
was evening. The sun was fading away in a golden mist. Upon a
ndah beneath the shade of the blossoming vanilla a young creole wo-
 was enjoying the cool evening She was a mother for the first time
the mysterious feeling of maternity thrilled her heart. She looked
nto the heavens dreamily, when suddenly she heard a piercing cry,
 a stifled sigh. For an instant she listened, then with a smile she bent
 the odor of a rose. In this attitude she was beautiful as the Mad-
n.
pregnant negress had been tied to a ladder and they were whipping
poetically by the light of the setting sun. Do you know what she had
 ? She had broken a saucer. They had to take a round out of the
er to make room for the bosom where the Almighty had deposited a

VI.

ire, you go regularly to church every Sunday. You must consent
efore, out of respect to the gospel, to allow the slave to become, if not a
, at least a christian. Let him be baptised in the name of the Father, the
, and the Holy Ghost, and by virtue of his baptism he will be granted a
e in the city of the dead and equality in paradise. But there is a slight
wback which you did not at first foresee, in that the Bible constitutes the
le Protestant worship. You should therefore, Sire, as a Protestant,
h the slave to read so as to make him a good christian. But when he
ns to read what will he read?
ou may refuse to allow the slave to exercise his intelligence, but you
not root this intelligence out of his brain. His intellect works even un-
the yoke, although confusedly as though under a fog What would it
hen—were his mind to become educated and were he to learn that
were no better than himself, and say to you let it be decided between
Man to man !
ou foresaw the danger of this, and in order to avert it you made his
rance the safeguard of slavery. Keeping the slave in ignorance, Sire,
has been your policy. You have closed the schools to the negro, and
 hidden the alphabet from him. The Scythians put out the bodily eyes
eir slaves as a prudential measure ; but you treat your slaves infinitely
 cruelly, for you put out their mental eyes; and the negro, who is crea-
after God's image like yourself, will go henceforth from the cradle to the
ve with night in his soul and night on his face.
ou have elevated him to christianity, probably that he may practice the
pel, and the gospel condemns promiscuousness. You take pains that the
ks shall intermarry, and a clergyman blesses their union. Why should it
lessed ? Rather let it be cursed and the woman be rendered barren, for

she will only bring forth heirs to slavery. And the children born of tl
love, whom she has nourished at her breast and cherished in her heart wh
will become of them when they reach a marketable age? The master w
send them to market, and marriage, the most moral of all institutions, l
comes but another torment added to slavery.

Without irony, let the inmates of the negro pen be considered simply
male and female; let them come together and bring forth after the lapse
nine months; let them mix indiscriminately; let the mmeet promiscuously a
then forget each other; this will do for negroes. Why have any marriag
at all? And the young white girl, Sire, your own daughter will recei
her education in this school. I say nothing of your son : I know alrea
what his first love affair will be.

Occasionally the slave takes to flight. In local phraseology, he vamose
The swamps are deserted and the underwood dense. By sleeping durir
the day and traveling at night, he may be able to gain the border. Wh
do you do to recapture him? You train up a pack of bloodhounds to tra
the runaway. The slave owner has a right to hunt him, and if he chooses
risk the thousand dollars represented by his human game, he may shoot
him, and kill him, — the law allows it.

And these nameless crimes, these insults to God and man, are not repu
nant to, and do not even astonish the gentle blue-eyed creoles, the wiv
and sisters of the knights of the whip! The frequency of their occurren
has to a great extent made them a normal state of affairs, an old establish
tradition, rendered legitimate by custom. What in fact is there to co
plain of in the negro's destiny? Does he not get enough to eat when he
hungry? Does he not dance at Christmas? Yes, eat or die, such is tl
lot; King Cotton has declared it. And if thou shouldst incautiously murmu
at thy portion, thy master will send thee to the plantation executioner wi
an order for fifty lashes, payable to bearer, and the official will pay them
sight without further formality.

You degrade the slave at pleasure; you put him up at auction on
block like butcher's meat. Draw near, here is a negro, or better still a n
gress; you may examine her at leisure, undress her, turn her round, di
cuss her price before her, stipulate against any hidden imperfection, ar
then take possession of the merchandise. If she groans and weeps you ma
take her away tied to the tail of your horse; the town of Raleigh in Nor
Carolina has witnessed such an act.

And after you have debased the negro, and corrupted him by his degr
dation, how, Sire, do you satisfy your conscience? You make the slav
himself responsible for the effects of slavery : you use his baseness as an a
gument to maintain him in servitude. But who has branded him with ign
miny except you, his master his second creator? And you have recourse to
second crime in order to justify the first.

You lower the negro to the level of a brute, and then you say that he is n
a man. And whose fault is this, I pray; He is not a man, you say; but
not the negress a woman? Yes, when she is young and well made—th
you condescend to prove. And the profit is all your own, for later you w
be able to sell your own child. A mulatto is more valuable than a fu
blooded African.

I will take your word for it that the negro is despicable; but there
one still more despicable than he, to wit; you, yourself, King Cotton. Tl
slave is debased, but you are cruel. Which is to be preferred, a vitiat
nature or crime? Moreover the negro is your work, and the work is a c
terion of the workman.

The slave being degraded by his master, degrades the latter in his tur

he master loses his sense of right and wrong; the planter does wrong
without even suspecting that he is doing so. The Cæsarian folly of des-
otism extinguishes the last symptom of conscience and kills remorse. He
candid in his own crime.

Immorality begets immorality. The burning soil of the South devours the
.borer, who can only live there about seven years upon an average. The
onsumption exceeds the supply, and slavery might die out for want of the
.w material; but in the border states, rejoicing in the "peculiar institution,"
ere are good fathers of families, prudently intent upon establishing their
us and endowing their daughters. These men will originate the ingenious
ea of profiting by the mildness of a temperate climate to breed up human
.ttle on a large scale.

The-e prudent men will seek out well-proportioned brood negresses who
ill produce first-class stock which they will subsequently dispose of further
uth at high rates. Sire, I congratulate you upon this stroke of genius :
u have invented a new sort of conscription. You may say, as another
ng once said : "I have so many men to spend upon my battle-field."

But the breeding district will not suffice to supply the slave-market ;
mething more will be required, and despite the law, despite the penalty
death provided by the law for the slaver captain, the Southron will bold-
keep up the slave trade in the open light of day. You will protect him
cretly ; you will interpose your authority between the criminal and the
llows. When a cruiser brings to Charleston a slaver aptured in the ex-
cise of his vocation, the planter-judge will declare that he honest dealer
human flesh has been calumniated, and that he was sailing along the Af-
can coast for purely philanthropic purposes, solely in order to offer the
vantages of commerce to the black race.

But before long the farce of this underhand traffic, continually pursued
ith impunity, will prove too revolting to the uprightness of the South, and
me honest citizen will demand the reestablishment of the slave trade open-
and undisguisedly. This man merits mention. He is called Doctor Thor-
ll, and his name should be nailed like a rook to Jefferson Davis' door.

I do not say, Sire, that your Southern vassals are altogether bloodthirsty
n, of repulsive mien, whose clothes reek with the professional odor of
tchers. On the contrary, they are perfect gentlemen, agreeable, aimable,
d always ready to do the honors of their homes with smiling, constant
urtesy. They have debts, white hands, and good manners. They are
od hunters, riders, and pistol shots. They are fond of painting, music
d literature. They look upon labor as derogatory, therefore they do not
ork ; but they possess all the charms of aristocratic slothfulness, includ-
g good-breeding, good-taste, and well-lined purses.

Do not fear that they will ever doubt the rightfulness of slavery. Their
eologians of all denominations—and they are more subtle than the most
ly casuists of the old school of Ignatius Loyola—have long since re-
ved the conscience of the planter of all anxiety on this head. These
igion-mongers who, like Judas Iscariot, would sell Christ a second time,
en their Bible with a pious air, and through the assistance of the Holy
ost they discover that the Lord eternally empowers the white men of
uisiana to buy black flesh for their use, and to whip the same *ad libitum*.
Whenever a crime is committed in this world there will always be a crea-
re in clerical guise upon its trace, ready to canonize the deed and make
d have a hand in it. *Omnis potestas a Deo.* Your chaplain, Sire, has
doubt communicated this text to your august ear, and demonstrated to
u from the pulpit that you possess a right of life and death over your
low-creatures for the public welfare of Cotton.

VII.

Still, North America permitted matters to take their course. She see
to have good-naturedly consented to the scandal of a republic in two p:
with liberty inscribed upon one page of its constitution and slavery upon
other ; but liberty possesses such virtue in itself that if you link it to
vitude one of two results must ensue ; either servitude will stifle it, o
will efface the former.

The day was destined to come when men worthy of the name should
amine the conscience of the republic and demand whether the living p
dox of the "peculiar institution" should still longer dishonor the countr
Washington. A voice, low and indistinct at first, rises from Penn's col
pronouncing the word "abolition;" but timidly like a secret whispere
one's ear.

This first protest astonished, and then irritated even the immacu
North. Why raise thus unseasonably a difficulty of this nature? \
disturb the quiet of those who saw nothing and the peace of those who
not wish to see anything, of those who turned aside their heads and l
on their way? Therefore the people of Philadelphia grew indignant
set fire to the hall where abolitionism held its first meeting.

Then Channing began to speak, and by the evangelical serenity of
eloquence he gently brought North America to blush for this and to
monise her policy with that liberty decreed by the heart of man befo
was countersigned by the constitution. From that moment the aboli
party weighed in the balance of public opinion with all the weight of
tice.

But woe to the ingenuous apostle simple-minded enough to believe, t
under a *régime* of absolute liberty, he had a right to utter his opin
aloud in the streets. If, by chance, he had the impudence to show a
of respect for the "peculiar institution" or to assert casually that s'n
was perhaps not the beau-ideal of civilization, when in the land of good-b
ing, the home of your rich, fast planters, well gloved and curled, elega
Panama hats and white pantaloons, that very instant the unfortunate a
tionist found himself seized by the collar to be tarred and feathered in
State House ; for the knights of the lash are a jovial race and fond of a
in their idle moments. When they have no slaves to punish with t
lordly hands, they love to enjoy a free, hearty laugh, especially aft
"cocktail." They hold that since the days of Molière a man daubed
tar is the wittiest thing invented, and they repeat the joke *ad nauseam.*

Still, experience showed the relative value of free labor and slave la
While free labor in the north of America was incessantly invading the
derness, peopling the desert, drawing the stout sons of Europe to its ra
and jointly with them transforming a desert into a nation at every step,
vile labor, despite the development of the cultivation of cotton, and
withstanding that it monopolized the European markets, was barely ena
to keep a people, burdened with debt, at the same level during the s
period. With progress on the one hand and stagnation on the other
result the following consequence.

The Senate represents the States. So many states send so many Sena
whatever be their population ; but owing to the increasing flow of emi
tion the North was alone able to improvise new states and consequentl
send new Senators to Congress. The North, therefore, year after year,
a majority in the Senate ; and as the section inclined more and more tov
abolitionism, the day drew near to put the slavery question to the vote.

What did the South do in order to restore the equilibrium and retain the majority? Being unable to create new states by their labor, they essayed to conquer such by dint of arms and to sow slavery by force. Thus they got up the Mexican expedition and imposed involuntary labor upon Texas. Labor in vain, the North was always ahead.

The South, feeling that their human property was in danger, thought fit to play a bold game, and on their part to threaten to split the republic in vain. They thus succeeded in obtaining from the easy-going good-natured North, first the Missouri compromise, then its violation, then the extradition law, then the decision of the United States Court placing slave property on a footing with all other kinds of property in every state in the union. This amounted to rendering slavery universal. The South went so far. Destiny looked on and cried, Halt!

VIII.

But one day an honest man named John Brown tried to discover whether there were any pulsation left beneath the negro's cotton shirt. This was an error, I admit. You seized the noble champion of humanity, you tried him and you hung him. Bravo, Sire, I recognize you by this act of clemency, for you could have burnt him alive at the stake! But when he was executed a great shudder swept through the North of America. Thenceforth the sacred cause of abolitionism was invested with the halo of martyrdom.

It had already sounded its tocsin, in the shape of a paltry little book written by a woman; and it was less than a book, it was a novel. You smiled compassionately at it, did you not? Your children may cry over it for a long while. America read Mrs. Stowe's elegy and bewailed her state; and the presidency of Abraham Lincoln sprang from the presidency of Uncle Tom.

I breathe again. I have rid me of a nightmare, for the time for justice has arrived: right is not a lie. Scarcely had the South learned the election of Lincoln before with their impious hand, already polluted with the blood of the slave, they dared to strike their mother, to strangle the Constitution, throwing to the winds the common glory of their common country, telling the Union their intention to walk thenceforward independently with the negro trampled beneath their feet.

You, Sire, and you alone, without provocation or excuse, have broken the compact which you signed and swore to keep. In your rebellious folly you said to yourself, "What have I to fear from the North, from the lovers of peace and dollars? Will they dare to raise an army for the abstract satisfaction of unity? And supposing that they dare, I need only hold fast to my bales of cotton. At one blow I can cause a famine in all the markets of Europe, and array all the spindles and looms of Manchester and Mulhouse against these fanatical Yankees, and their Constitution. Then England and France must of necessity,—either jointly or separately—intervene in favor of slavery in order to save their cotton.

And if they hesitate, if they shrink from armed mediation, what will they do with their disbanded hosts of cotton spinners? Will they be allowed to wander at random, pale and ragged, like the spectres of famine, about the extinguished furnaces and silent factories, until at last, tired of suffering they make one desperate effort and throw themselves upon the bayonets of their countrymen? Certainly not; France as well as England must prefer to open the Southern markets at any cost, even by force of shot and shell.

This is the impious calculation you made when you rebelled again
he Constitution. You condemned the poorer classes of Europe to want f
work, in other words, to a slow death, so as to preserve slavery in all i
purity ; after adding another crime to your list, you hauled down the feder
flag waving over Fort Sumter.

During the last ten years, Sire, you have been silently preparing for civ
war. You furnished the first example of a conspirator in the Cabinet. Yo
have overspread the South with an immense network of rabid democrac
long since you organized the secret society of the Knights of the Golde
Circle, the three golden circles inclosed the one within the other, with a
the dexterity of a Chinese puzzle. The first was to separate the se
ond, and the second the third, and the countersign passed from one to th
other without the possibility of discovering who had given it.

You chose your time well. The Constitution places an interval of thre
months between the election of the President and his inauguration ; durin
that period, Buchanan was finishing his presidential term, like a gloom
sunset. He was a man after your own heart, a mind devoted to sl
very, a magnetic needle turned to the South pole instead of towar
the North, and he conscientiously employed the balance of his presiden
in betraying the Union.

Treason is perhaps too forcible an expression—he was not exactly
traitor. But when the rebellion boldly declared itself, when civil war w
openly begun, Buchanan was most conveniently affected with a wilful dim
ness of ocular and mental vision ; he saw nothing, and knew nothing. B
sent all the Northern ordnance to the South ; he sent the army to th
Western frontier in order to prevent the imminent invasion of a dozen red
skins who threatened to pillage the New York banks.

Thus you had three months start of the North. You took them unaware
You had them within range, you had an army while they had but militi
They rushed heedlessly against you at Bull Run, and you butchered them
So there was nothing left but to admit the defeat and beg for mercy!

By no means ! While still under the first shock of the disaster, this peac
ful laborious people, thus villainously attacked and abominably massacre
in ambuscades, sent back a shout of defiance, and staked everything in t
struggle, to its last man and its last dollar.

Heroism is contagious. America offered so magnificent a spectacle
right-minded Europeans, that young princes, ignorant of democracy throug
the accident of their birth, deemed it an honor to win their spurs benea
the banner of the Republic. The fact is greatly to their credit ; I say
without flattery, for between their principles and our principles, lies th
broad Atlantic. For their account I hope, that while serving under th
star-spangled banner, they may have learned that there is something hig
er than princes, that there is the citizen.

IX.

During this time, Sire, you sent agents to Europe to decoy public opi
ion to the side of slavery. Your legates *à latere* are at this moment di
pensing a prodigious amount of philanthropy. They say, or make othe
say, in affecting tones ; see, blood is being poured out like water ; battl
constantly succeed each other and always without result ; after two yea
slaughter in line upon the banks of the Potomac the North has been unab
to advance a step without falling back immediately afterward. The ma

ie nations of Europe should throw themselves between the combatants
imitation of the Sabines. The interests of humanity are at stake as well
your industrial interests.

This is what the missionaries from the South preach to the four corners
he earth. Do not delude yourself, Sire. Despite the suffering that your frat-
dal struggle inflicts upon our country. you will not succeed in pervert-
public opinion ; you may try every avenue of publicity, but you will
y find fickle partisans and doubtful friends of freedom. We have seen
m at work, we know their record ; they like your despotism, not that
y uphold slavery, for its name frightens them ; they would condemn the
perty and glorify the owner.

Vith such as these there can be no discussion ; they are known and re-
d. There are, however, in the ranks of the French press, partisans
iberty like ourselves, who think themselves able to defend what they
the principle of secession without offence to liberty. They say honest-
hat, with ourselves, they reject slavery in principle—with this addition,
the American republic is not a State, that it is a juxta-position of States,
h of which has the right to withdraw from the Union and take its star
u the flag.

he American republic not a State ! Verily, we must be asleep with our
open. According to this, Holland also was not a state in the seven-
th century ! Then Switzerland too, is not a nation at this hour of her
ory ; and when General Dufour crushed the Sonderbund insurrection, he
mitted in reality the same crime that Catherine was guilty of toward
and !

What ! The North and the South of America one memorable day in
last century by common consent threw off the supremacy of the mother
ntry, to enjoy it entirely in common ; they voted a federal constitution
ommon ; they built a federal capitol in common, where they instal and
nize a federal legislative system in common and a federal presidency, a
ral administration, a federal diplomacy, a federal army and navy, a fed-
mint, and later jointly also, they bought Louisiana from France and
ida from Spain with federal money, and again out of federal funds they
ed forts and built arsenals for the universal defence of all their frontiers,
yet they are not a State, nor even a nation, but simply a handful of
which the first gust of wind may disperse !

ead the constitution over again ! There you will see that the thirteen
inal states entered into a solemn agreement each one with the other, to
always one single national body. As long as the South held a majori-
the republic, (and as a consequence of such majority the monopoly
e presidency, and with the presidency the disposal of the federal offices,
elcome gift for distribution among their party leaders) they never
med, that I know, of disputing the sacredness of the contract, or of
esting the legitimacy of a power which they monopolized for their ad-
tage, and enjoyed among themselves.

nd now that luck is against them, when they are in a minority, when
the turn of the North to hold the presidency, after legally gaining it,
South complains of overbearing. They held the place long but now
are told to leave and make room for another. The grandee's honor is
lted : he puts on his hat and leaves in a rage, nothing but a duel to the
h can avenge the affront.

X.

Since when has it been optional with one party to an agreement to a
nul the contract without the consent of the other party ? A contract is e
tered into precisely in order to prevent such a contingency. Otherwi
there would never be any treaty in the world and man's hand-writin
would be but a writing upon sand. The fate of the world would be conti
ually dependent upon the peculiar system of pitch and toss called milita
science.

Why was the thing called a constitution thought of, unless in order
prevent what the South is doing at this moment. Every nation, even whe
self-styled one and indivisible, must always run the risk of domestic qua
rels ; and there are but two means to decide the difference, war or the ba
lot box.

When war is resorted to the stronger crushes down the weaker until t
latter rises up and crushes the conqueror in his turn—and thus war bege
war without end, until the country after tearing itself to pieces with its ow
hands, expires in a convulsion of anarchy and disappears in a conquest.

If it is to be settled by the constitution, then, instead of appealing to t
sword the verdict of public opinion will be sought : the struggle will l
definitively settled by suffrage. The minority will respectfully agree to t
decision of the majority as the expression of justice. This is a simple fi
tion for the benefit of the common weal, implying no irrevocable decre
for, according to the constitution itself, the minority always possess t
right of reconsidering the subject before the people when what is lackin
may be recovered.

Hitherto this has been the great rule in politics. But the South thoug
fit to make an exception. They willingly approved the ballot box when
gave them a majority, but when they found themselves in a minority the
took up the musket. We must certainly admit the right to revolt or el
proclaim the inviolability of tyranny, but recourse to force can never ra
as a system. It can only be resorted to as a forlorn hope, and there mu
exist the sacred incentive of freedom to be gained in order to justify an u
right man in assuming the tragical responsibility of a revolution.

But when all the advantages of liberty are combined, when a people a
thus above public opinion, and with every means of redress at hand, wh
right can they hope to obtain by victory which they do not already po
sess ? One of the best and most deserving features of the American Co
stitution is that it lends no species of plea for insurrection. Why, for i
stance, should the people of Illinois declare war against the Union, whe
the Union oppresses liberty in no section, but on the contrary everywhe
guarantees it.

And yet, Sire, you have unsheathed the sword, and why? Had the n
gro race not been in existence you would not have dreamed of rebellin
for your rebellion will not give you a single additional right or guarante
You have revolted for one object only, the maintenance of slaver
Hitherto nations have rebelled for liberty alone. Your subjects, Sire, w
be the first that have risen to support despotism.

Your keep up your rebellion by means worthy of its origin. I do not a
lude to the reign of terror that you have created at home in order to sti
he murmurings of the loyal partisans of the Union who still look wistfu
in the direction of their common home. Nor will I refer to the terrib
cannibalism which a certain young Belgian *savant* has depicted in all i

errible truthfulness. You have closed the door upon us, Sire, and hidden ourself from our sight. You are modest regarding your handiwork, leav ng its perfections to be inferred rather than admired.

I speak only of your open and avowed acts; of your barbarous proclam tions unworthy of Ghengis-Kan in which you condemned Union Generals nd negro soldiers to the halter. And this is not merely a threat, for you ave already carried the sentence into effect. Still you had a scruple; you ight have simply hanged your black prisoners; but you preferred to shoot em. This is shorter and more honorable. Sire, your conduct is hor ble.

After this what can it serve to mention the Alabama, a corsair that lunders and then sinks every merchant vessel in her path, brazenly violat g the first law of privateering, for even privateering has its laws. We ote this, Sire, and we see by your conduct that you are really the pirate ing that rumor terms you. By your present acts we see that you need ypocrisy in order to wheedle some European power into an alliance. We an foresee to what extent you would carry your filibustering if victory ould obliterate your revolt. You lay down the mask too soon, Sire. I espise you, for you lack sense.

XI.

I know that there are men among us who feel a natural antipathy to the ankee race. How can they like a people who never laugh and hardly nile, who speak but little and meditate eternally? What merit can be ranted to a morose race who have, up to the present, failed to produce an ctress or a milliner of any note, or even a racy specimen of their literature? hey chew, smoke, and spit, and sit with their heels on the mantel-piece. ow disgusting a spectacle to the goddess of liberty. At the theatre when ey ought to hiss they applaud, and when they should applaud they hiss. not this turning the world upside down? You will soon see them wear g white mourning like the Chinese. And how about this democratic uality where one has but one seat in a steamboat or railroad car, where e millionaire must sit side by side with his bootblack! A certain French dy, tolerably well known in print, even goes so far as to affirm that the ankee sleeps with his boots on. Pray how do you know, madam? Did you ok under the counterpane?

The Yankee, I admit, possesses the defect of being a meditative man. e is as taciturn as the Western wilderness. He does not slap you on the oulder at the first meeting; he does not jump into familiarity at the sec d; he does not borrow a dollar or your wife the third time he sees u; but is this a fair reason why one should set one'sself against right, cause the Yankee happens to represent right, dry and unadorned. And it not an evidence of being prejudiced against right when you place the orth and the South on a footing of equality? Peace is desirable in the terest of humanity, we are told. Undoubtedly it is to be desired; but w is it to be obtained?

Can it be secured by recognizing the schism of the South as a perfected t, and by advising the North to accept this basis? This view of the estion would encourage the South to continue the war; it would lead em to believe that they were secretly supported by some great European tion; and further, it would be an unmerited blow to the North, legaliz g rebellion by I know not what sort of diplomatic chicanery.

When an established government permits foreign intervention betwee
the constitution which it should defend, and a portion of its people in r
bellion against this constitution, it does not negociate; it resigns its righ
as England would have done had she accepted the mediation of Austria
the time of Edward's expedition in Scotland. But the North, irritated a
humiliated as they are by the results hitherto of this traitorous war, so
confident and firm in their sense of right, will spend ten years of here
fighting and ten thousand millions of money, before they will consent
forfeit these rights, or admit that they are in any degree in the wrong.

If a speedy peace is wished for, the South must be placed beyond the pa
of public opinion. A moral blockade is necessary. One must turn asi
and say, I do not know you; you may win battles and shoot negroes, y
may burn defenceless vessels, you may be able to accomplish all of whi
unbridled force is capable: you may do all this, but you cannot enlist t
sympathies of a single honest man in Europe.

This state of "coventry" would have checked the arrogance of the Sout
and reacted upon the popular mind in the long run. The secret oppositi
of a portion of the Southern people would gradually have grown in strengt
and finally the majority would have comprehended that they were the ma
stay of this terrible tragedy. A war for what object? To maintain s
very for the benefit of one hundred thousand planters, deeply indebted a
mortgaged to the North, and who find it convenient at present to pay th
debts with musket balls.

The South cannot conquer. They have gained temporary advantage
but at this moment their armies are harmless and hemmed in beyond t
possibility of escape. The South has to face a terrible enemy, one th
strikes incessantly, and destroys them in detail. This enemy is Tim
Every day exhausts them more and more. They are only able to carry
the war now, by conscription and paper money; they have no longer a
revenue or products, and the grass grows in more than one city in yo
kingdom.

The abolition of slavery has given the rebellion its death-blow. T
Southerners may point a pistol at the heart of every negro; but the sacr
leaven of liberty will act—with greater or less rapidity, doubtless—yet
is destined in one way or another to work upon the minds of the enslav
race, and at this moment more than one negro is thinking of the northe
bank of the Potomac, with his ear to the earth to catch the sound of t
Federal artillery.

And as an opportunity now offers, I crave leave to render my homage
the patient genius of Mr. Lincoln. In France we have an incurable passi
for theatrical effect in politics: we deem it fashionable to sneer at the e
ergetic slowness of the Yankee President. Being unable, with our Gall
temperament, to comprehend those phlematic natures, that grow great
under defeat than victory—like Coligny or William of Orange—we ask
ourselves why Mr. Lincoln signed the emancipation bill with two clause
the one decreeing the immediate, and the other the prospective abolition
slavery.

We reason as though Mr. Lincoln wielded a dictatorial, unrestrict
power at the White House, accounting solely to the God of his conscienc
But Mr. Lincoln simply presides over a republic where popular opini
rules, and he is surrounded by divers opinions upon the question of sl
very The democratic party wish to uphold it, and the republicans desi
to abolish it, therefore Mr. Lincoln waits, with an eye fixed upon each si
of the scale.

XII.

No one knows better than Mr. Lincoln how to utilize defeat. When, by bold victory, the South provoked the North to recognize the necessity of emancipation, Mr. Lincoln at once yielded and made a step forward. And like manner, after the disaster at Chæronea, the Lincoln of Athens, did away with slavery, and when a slave thanked him he answered, you owe your freedom not to me but to Chæronea. I borrow this historical incident from Mr. Agénor de Gasparin's eloquent work.

I have faith in Lincoln, I believe in the old rail-splitter. At this moment he holds a world in his hand, and I hope that he will not let it fall; but impossible as it seems, if, at some future day the North should mistrust itself and regret the old state of affairs in the past, what could such an act of weakness effect? The artery once opened, its tide could be arrested for an instant only.

I will even admit the hypothesis that the North may confess its powerlessness and say to the slave-whippers, to the rag-pickers of the Constitution, I have thrown it into their basket as though it were an old rag, I am wrong, and I am sorry. Let us call our witnesses and amicably establish respective frontiers.

But where will you place the boundary? Perhaps you will lay it down along the line of the Potomac, a line so often won and lost, and watered with human blood, or by the long trail of the five hundred thousand corpses that were once fathers, sons, brothers, men loving and beloved, who lie rotting now because the gentlemen of South Carolina thought fit one day to commit a double crime; a crime against humanity and a crime against their country.

You will set your stakes across this cemetery, above the almost uncovered bones mouldering there; but sink them as deep as you may, they will not hold. You will sign a peace, but you will not have it; for beneath the very feet of the plenipotentiaries this tragic soil, choked with the dead, will yawn open to yield up the spectres of the Bull Run victims. In the absence of the living, the dead will rise to protest against this embrace between the aggressive South and the victimized North.

And think you that a few signatures written down side by side on a sheet of paper, will suffice to efface the recollection of this terrible slaughter. No, these reminiscences will remain written upon men's hearts in letters of fire and blood, and the widows in the most distant villages of the West will water them with their tears by their firesides and at their work.

North and South, you will ever regard each other with an angry eye. At the first opportunity you will break out again; there will be another slaughter house on the face of the earth, and the new world will have nothing to envy the old. Henceforward you must go armed and each keep up an army of four hundred thousand soldiers. You will attempt to avoid a momentary expense by a patched-up peace and before the end of the century your national debt will have reached two hundred or three hundred thousand millions. This is the ordinary cost of an army during one generation. If you doubt it inquire of Austria.

The day that a permanent army shall exist in North America, you may bid adieu to liberty, as it has been accepted and practised hitherto. With the danger of foreign war will come the doctrine of public safety, and governments will be made and unmade with the bayonet, as in Buenos Ayres. I cannot see how the commerce of Europe is to profit by this.

XIII.

Should Europe, however, entertain the unfortunate idea of creating wi[?]
her own hand, in the Gulf of Mexico, a cotton republic, a black state found[?]
upon slavery, such a rash act would inflict upon the world an element [?]
perturbation and a scourge more terrible than the cholera. Once master [?]
its own movements, this pro-slavery government, this despicable and a[?]
cursed political monstrosity, repulsive to the entire world, would speedi[?]
bid defiance to everything, aggravating in order to diminish the horror [?]
its crime, and would become so powerful that it would finally comma[?]
respect.

It would not be as in the past a disgraceful underhand attack up[?]
Texas or Cuba ; it would be piracy exercised on a grand scale in order [?]
render slavery universal. The slave trade would be carried on for reaso[?]
of state, and carried on in a royal manner by squadrons of vessels. Fro[?]
that day the negro would eternally wear the mourning of civilization up[?]
his brow.

But, whatever may happen, I hope that France, the offspring of revo[?]
tion, will never lend a hand to such an anachronism, and one so inconsiste[?]
with her past history ; did not the French revolution inaugurate neg[?]
emancipation and first grant the black the right of citizenship ? And [?]
one reminiscence calls up others, I beg leave to mention here an incident [?]
the present time, although it is already so distant that it seems like t[?]
past.

It was in February. Revolution was everywhere at work, and throug[?]
out Europe every instant a fresh explosion announced the fall of anoth[?]
kingdom. All Paris was on foot ; the streets were alive ; and clouds [?]
smoke floated in the air. The wind was laden with words as though an i[?]
visible spirit spoke in the mist. The crowd marched restlessly and excite[?]
ly from street to street with colors flying and drums beating, paradi[?]
their chimera and their hope ; their truth or their dream.

But above this agitated, swaying sea of humanity, above its uproar a[?]
tumult, in the calm region of high inspirations and sacred desires, the n[?]
republic, serene and holy, looked mentally beyond the sea. Full of t[?]
love of human dignity and everywhere present where there was a wou[?]
to heal, the new republic drew up the decree abolishing slavery, and t[?]
eleven members of the provisional government signed it. When the la[?]
signer laid down his pen they threw themselves into each other's arms a[?]
embraced with all the joy of the workmen of humanity after doing a go[?]
act.

Ah ! the men, whoever they were, who signed that decree may be forg[?]
ten now, but their short term of power was not spent in vain. Had [?]
king signed it, such a decree would have sufficed to make his reign glo[?]
ous The provisional government were not even allowed the credit of [?]
Serve humanity and such will be your reward ! But the good was [?]
complished and it remains. The divine spirit has also its day in our co[?]
try, and if this day is drawing to its close, there are at least others beyo[?]
the ocean to whom the last revolution has given the right to shout [?]
Liberty !

This, Sire, is what I had to say to Your Majesty. I have finished ; [?]
let me give you a parting word of advice. I will not appeal to your hea[?]
for that would be speaking to the absent : I will appeal simply to yo[?]
interests, then I may have some chance of fixing your attention.

lieve me and tempt destiny no longer. Remember the example of the
ch nobility. They left the soil rather than submit to common law, and
soil passed from them into the hands of a class sprung from revolution
identified with liberty. Since that day the French nation has formed
family. I leave you to meditate, Sire, upon this lesson of history.
ow many vassals have you in reality? Scarcely a hundred thousand.
se alone are guilty of the insurrection. All that will be necessary will
turn their plantations into money and introduce the population of
West into this regenerated section. This is the way to solve the sla-
question and effect the reconciliation of the South. And now, Sire, I
God to have you in his keeping, to correct you and incline you to-
d repentance. Amend, Sire, otherwise one may soon see in Paris a
ged old man asking the police for a passport in order to follow the
e of Modena to Venice. That old man will be King Cotton.

THE END.

Messager Franco-Américain Printing Office, 51, Liberty street, New York.

LaVergne, TN USA
02 November 2009
162819LV00004B